The light wakes Ricky up.

The world wakes up, too.

Morning

What time is it?

It is morning. Ricky feels hungry.

It is time for breakfast.

After the night, the air is cold.

But the sun warms up the world.

People get ready for the day.

Day

What time is it?

In the daytime, Ricky is at school. He is a busy bee.

In the daytime, Ricky's mum
and dad are busy at work.

Noon

What time is it?

It is noon, the middle of the day.

The sun is high in the sky.

What time is it?

After noon, it is the afternoon!
After school, there is still
lots of time for Ricky to play.

Sunset

What time is it?

It is sunset. The sun goes down and day turns to night.

After sunset, it is dusk. The light fades away.

Evening

What time is it?

It is evening. In summer, days are long. Ricky plays outside after dinner.

In winter, days are short.

Ricky comes inside early.

Dad comes home in the dark.

Night

What time is it?

It is night. It is dark outside.
Inside, lights help Ricky
to read.

At night, it is cold outside.

But it is warm inside.

The world goes quiet.

Bedtime

What time is it?

It is time for bed. At night, many animals sleep, too.

Ricky likes to watch the moon. Like the sun, the moon moves slowly across the sky.

Midnight

What time is it?

It is midnight. Ricky is asleep, but this owl is awake.

It hunts for food in the dark.

At night, some people are at work.

This garage is open all night.

Night and day

What time is it?

It is morning.

The birds are singing in the trees.

Night turns to day,
and day turns to night.
Every day!

Here are some words about time.

Sunrise

Morning

Afternoon

Sunset

Night

Here are some words about day
and night.

Play

Breakfast

School

Sleep

Can you write
a story with these words?

Do you know?

There are 24 hours in a whole day.

That means a day and a night.

Midnight
12 a.m.

Early morning
5 a.m.

Morning
8 a.m.

Noon
12 p.m.

Afternoon
5 p.m.

Evening
8 p.m.

The hours before noon are a.m.

The hours after noon are p.m.